THE STORY OF GIO

From the Heike Monogatari
Retold by Ridgely Torrence

First published in 1935

Published by Left of Brain Books

Copyright © 2023 Left of Brain Books

ISBN 978-1-396-32598-4

First Edition

All rights reserved. No part of this publication may be reproduced, distributed, or transmitted in any form or by any means, including photocopying, recording, or other electronic or mechanical methods, without the prior written permission of the publisher, except in the case of brief quotations permitted by copyright law. Left of Brain Books is a division of Left Of Brain Onboarding Pty Ltd.

PUBLISHER'S PREFACE

About the Book

"The Story of Gio from the Heike Monogatari, retold by Ridgely Torrence [1935]."

(Quote from sacred-texts.com)

CONTENTS

PUBLISHER'S PREFACE
FOREWORD 1
    THE STORY OF GIO 4

FOREWORD

EXCEPT for obvious differences in local color and religious background the Mediaeval romances of Japan are much like those of Europe. Brave knights perform incredible feats of valor, wicked tyrants are circumvented or overthrown, supernatural influences play their good or evil parts, and sometimes distressed damsels, as in the tragic little story here retold, give up the quest of worldly happiness and resign themselves to lives of prayer. The chief differences are these: the frequency of suicide, for in the Orient the Almighty did not fix His canon 'gainst self-slaughter; the position of women in a civilization that knew nothing of the Mariolatry of our Middle Ages; and a weakening of the motive of love between the sexes, which is counterbalanced by an increased emphasis on the loyalty between squire and knight, knight and overlord, and above all on the loyalty of wife to husband.

The Heike Monogatari, or Tales of the Heike Clan who were all-powerful until the vices of their leader Kiyomori assisted the brave young warriors of the Taira to overthrow them, were being sung to musical accompaniment by the middle of the 13th Century. There were numerous versions; and, as in the case of the Homeric poems, later redactions probably show traces of composite origin. One version seems to be as complete and unified as Sir Thomas Mallory's Morte d'Arthur, and from this the episode of the two dancing girls, Gio Gozen and Hotoke Gozen, has been translated for separate publication by the Japan Society.

It might have been possible to reprint the story from the only complete version of the Heike Monogatari existing in English--that of Professor A. L. Sadler, published in the Transactions of the Asiatic Society of Japan Vol. XLVI, Part II; but it seemed to the Committee in charge that the use of this very scholarly translation, filled as it is with exact terms literally rendered, would make the pathos and the beauty of the tale, now first retold for itself alone, less easy of access to readers who care rather for literature and life than. for exactness of rendition; and under the expert guidance of Professor R. Tsunoda, Curator of the Japanese Library at Columbia University, an entirely new literal translation was prepared for us by Miss Helen B. Chapin whose work then. was given over to an alchemist and transmuted into the gold of simple English prose.

The illustration used as a frontispiece seems to have drawn its inspiration from a version of the story in which Gio sat beside Kiyomori while Hotoke danced; and the costume of the dancer is not quite that described in our text. It is, however, the best known and perhaps the most beautiful pictorial representation of the episode; and that details of costume as well as of text may have changed in the course of centuries is not surprising. The actual scene depicted is supposed to have occurred in the latter part of the 12th Century. The print was issued for New Years of 1765 and contains calendar marks for that year. It is thought to have been designed by Harunobu, the most brilliant as well as the most exquisite Ukiyo-ye artist of that time, and the fact that it bears the signature and seal of Kyosen--the patron or central figure of a group of artists to which Harunobu belonged--does not necessarily invalidate that supposition.

The thanks of the Committee are due to Dr. Tsunoda, Miss Chapin and Mr. Torrence, and are given with sincere appreciation.

L. V. L.

New York, November 1934

THE STORY OF GIO

THE voice of the great bell in the First Monastery of the Master intones the domination of eternal change over all that is.

The Bo tree, under which the Blessed One attained Enlightenment, foretells, with the glory of its petals, that they who rise up in splendor shall go down again into the ground.

The vain, the haughty glow for an instant, then like a vision, like a dream in April, at twilight, they pass, they fade.

Shorn of power, in the end, the strong, the victorious are cut down. They vanish like dust that is blown away.

IN the chronicles of distant lands there are records of various rulers who turned their faces from the commonweal. Intemperate, seekers after their own pleasure, careless of justice, blind to the evil in their realms, refusing to know the sorrows of their people, they did not survive their hour but were destroyed and faded wholly from the earth.

And in our own country it is well known that many have been tyrannous and shameless, but if we weigh justly the accounts of the Prime Minister Kiyomori, Prince, Priest and Regent, it is apparent that he surpassed them all, both by his edicts and his personal demeanor.

It was particularly at the height of his power, when the whole country lay helpless in his grasp, that he showed the most open contempt for the universal murmur against him, completely disregarding the people's adverse opinion. Such conduct as this bore fruit in most unusual and startling episodes, as, for instance that of the Shirabyoshi dancers.

There were, at that time, in the capital, two sisters, young Shirabyoshi girls who had practiced the art of that dance until their skill had become famous. Their mother had also been a Shirabyoshi and their names were Gio and Gijo.

Upon the elder girl, Gio, the Regent had for some time bestowed the favors of his love and Gijo, constantly in demand as an entertainer, drew from her audiences more than ordinary tribute. The Regent even provided for their mother by building her a good house and settling upon her a monthly income of five hundred bushels of rice and a large amount of money. So, lifted to great wealth and conspicuous position, the family was enrolled among the rarest favorites of fortune.

Now as to Shirabyoshi, the dance in which the sisters excelled, it was introduced in our country by two girls, Shima-no-Senzai and Waka-no-mae in the reign of the Emperor Toba-no-in. At first the dancers wore a formal kind of hunting costume, with divided skirts, all of white silk, with a white sheathed dirk in the sash and a black lacquered gauze hat. This hunter's garment caused it to be known as "the man's dance." But when the dance was half completed, the hat and the dirk were discarded and only the white costume was worn, which gave the dancers the name of Shirabyoshi, or White-Robed Rhythms.

There were many White-Robed Rhythm dancers in the capital and when the news of Gio's good fortune spread among them they received it in various ways. Though there were some whose envy of her was at least mingled with admiration, others felt toward her only a jealous hate. The envious admirers would say, "Ah how fortunate is Gio. If we become dancing courtesans like her we may win the same success. Perhaps by adding the syllable Gi to our names her good luck may also attend us. Let us add this syllable and see." So, one called herself Giichi, another Gini, still another Gifuku, another Gitoku and so the fashion spread. But the jealous ones said: "No, it is not a matter of the name, nor of any way in which it is spoken. Those who inherit luck from previous existence are born lucky;" and few of them added the syllable to their names.

So three years passed. Then a day came when the people of all classes in the capital began to praise a new Shirabyoshi dancer from Kaga province, a girl of sixteen named Hotoke.

Everyone who saw her declared that of all the many Shirabyoshi who had appeared before them, none had danced so well.

Such universal approval brought Hotoke at last to meditate upon her career and she said to herself, "My triumph will never be complete until I am summoned to dance before the Regent himself, the fountain-head of all good fortune. And since he has sent me no invitation, why should I not go without one, as entertainers are accustomed to do?" And she immediately went to the palace where she was conducted to a room adjoining that in which the Regent sat with Gio. Entering the Presence the servant announced: "The favorite dancer of the capital, Hotoke, has arrived seeking an audience."

Hearing this the Regent cried out in a high temper, "What is this! These players only appear by command! She dares to come without bidding? If her name were God or Buddha she should not see me while Gio is here. Send her away."

Wounded by these cruel words, Hotoke had started silently to withdraw when Gio spoke. "No," she protested, "it is an old custom for players to appear without invitation. And she is very young! It was only a thoughtless impulse of youth that brought her here. It would be cruel to turn her away with harsh words. Shame and distress would follow her out. I can so easily imagine myself in her place for I too once walked the same paths. Even if you will not see her dance and hear her songs, please relent and call her back for an audience. Then if you bid her go I shall be grateful for your generosity."

"Indeed!" returned the Regent, "Then solely to please you, I will see her and dismiss her" and he sent a servant with the summons.

The stricken Hotoke had already entered her carriage and was leaving the precinct but upon receiving the summons, she returned.

The Regent kept her waiting for some time before he appeared, now unattended by Gio, "So, you are Hotoke," he said, when his first careless glance had grown to a keener gaze, "I had not the least intention of seeing you today. But Gio pleaded so earnestly for your cause, that I decided at last to grant you an audience. And now that I have looked upon you, I find in me a desire to hear your voice. Sing me first an Imayo song." (the Imayo being a song in eight or twelve phrases of seven and five syllables).

And this was her song:

> "A delicate young pine at her first meeting
> With him who is her Lord, through joys and tears
> Sings of her hope that he may hear the beating

> Wings of the passage of a thousand years;
> While storks upon the tortoise island stand
> And crowd the lily pond to seek his hand."

The song was a most auspicious greeting at the first interview, storks, turtles and pines all being symbols of long life and the young pine being Hotoke herself.

Ravished by her singing and her beauty, the listeners urged her to repeat the song until she had sung it three times.

"And now my lady," the voice of the Regent followed the applause, "since you have shown yourself such an artist in Imayo, your dancing should be equally good. Let us see you dance. Call the hand-drum players."

Then with the drummers beating their measures Hotoke danced. And first, through the unfoldings of her art, the glory of her hair dawned upon the watchers, next the beauty of her face appeared to them and last, the marvel of all her graces, unsurpassed on earth, was displayed to the enchanted audience.

With gifts like these added to the natural excellence of her voice and its exquisite cultivation, how could she fail in her art? She danced with a perfection unimagined by the Regent, who continued to gaze at her in rapture.

His heart had turned wholly to Hotoke.

"What is this?" she exclaimed, reading in his manner the intensity of his mood. "First I came uninvited and you sent me away. Only through Gio's kindness I was brought back. Please allow me to go at once."

"Your plea," replied the Regent, "is rejected. But if your hesitation is due to Gio; if her presence here embarrasses you, I will dismiss her."

"How could you bring yourself to suggest such a thing?"

Hotoke protested. "Even if we were both to be kept here together I should be ashamed. But if you dismiss her and keep me here alone, she will suffer pain far deeper than shame."

"If that is the way you feel," was the Regent's answer, "Gio shall go at once" and he sent a messenger to Gio with the command, impatiently repeating it a little later by another messenger and not long after by a third.

Although Gio had often brooded on the probability of such an ending she never fixed its date in any present but only vaguely in some future day. But since the Regent's command was absolute and he continued to send it again and again she had no choice but to set her apartments in order and go.

Even those who stay briefly in the shade of the same tree or who meet once at the same fountain feel a certain sadness at parting. For such contacts mirror and echo moments in past existences. But she, whose life for three years had grown to be one with the Regent's felt far deeper sorrow than these.

Yet she saw, in her grief and regret, through the mist of her tears, that they were unavailing. She knew she must go and she left the palace.

Before she quitted her apartments, however, she wandered about in them, gathering up her many memories of one who was now lost to her and last of all she wrote some verses on the wall.

> "Whether the moor-flowers blossom long or late
> Or lay untimely down their colored freight
> Autumn shall yield them all an equal fate."

Then, taking her carriage, she went to her mother's home, where., in an inner room she gave herself up utterly to her tears. Seeing her condition her mother and sister plied her with questions and entreaties to which she made no reply and it was only from her maid that they drew a confession of what had happened.

As a result of the changed conditions, the monthly income of rice and money ceased and it was now the turn of the relations of Hotoke to taste the bliss of prosperity.

Rumors of these things soon spread until all the people of the capital, both masters and masses, began to ask, "Can it be true that Gio has been driven away from the palace? Then let us ask her to sing and dance for us."

Some sent letters and others messengers, but Gio, having no longer either heart or will to win further applause, refused to accept the letters or allow the messengers to communicate with her. Bound and helpless in the net of her unhappy memories, she shed her unavailing tears.

So that year passed. But in the next year's spring, the Regent sent a messenger to say: "How is Gio? And how are her affairs? Bid her come and sing Imayo songs and dance her dances to cheer Hotoke, who seems lonely."

To this Gio returned no answer but lay down with fresh tears at the new wound.

Finding her silent, the Regent bade the messenger to return and say, "Why does Gio send no word of her intentions? If she refuses to come, let her give her reason. I have a certain intention toward her." And he bade the messengers announce this, using the impersonal authority of the Regent's priestly title. The message, therefore, contained a sinister threat, "a certain intention" meaning that he planned some form of punishment.

Her mother, upon hearing this, began to entreat her: "Why do you send no answer, whether you will or will not go? Why not be warned by such a rebuke? "

"If I thought I should go," Gio's words rose through her tears, "then I would answer. But since I certainly shall not go, there is no answer. His message that he has 'a certain intention,' means without doubt that if I do not go, he is determined either to drive me out of the capital or put me to death. Beyond these two possibilities I have nothing to fear. But what if he should exile me from the city? I would feel no fresh sorrow at being set on such a path. And even if he should take my life, why should I grieve to be set free from my body? Once having been utterly rejected, why should I ever see his face again?"

Finding her still firm in her resolution of silence, the mother added her own tears to Gio's. "You must remember," she began again, "that the subjects of his realm cannot disobey the commands of the Regent. But far beyond this law are the laws that control us from former existences.

"The relation between man and woman is not one which begins in the life we are now living. Even of those who pledge to cling together for a thousand or ten thousand years, there are some who are soon parted.

"And again; a connection first supposed to be brief, sometimes lasts through life. The one most uncertain thing in the world is this relation between man and woman.

"Then too, the favors you have received during these past three years, have been so great that they should content you.

"It is true that if, after this summons, you refuse to go, you are still not likely to be put to death, but it is certain that you will be exiled from the capital. Then, even if you are driven out of the city, your sisters both are young and can easily find lodging places, however narrow, between rocks and the trees in the deep country. But I am too old to go and live in the country among strange surroundings. The thought of it saddens me deeply. I ask only that you perform the duties of filial piety for this world and the next by allowing me to finish my life in the city."

Upon hearing these words, unable to withstand any longer her mother's appeal, Gio rose and with the depths of her pitiful suffering apparent in her eyes, made ready to go.

To support her on the journey she took her sister Gijo with her, and attended by two other dancing girls the four went in a carriage to the palace.

Upon her arrival she was conducted not to the place that had formerly been hers, but to one far down in the lower part of the hall. "Alas," she said to herself, "Why should it be? No fault was found in me, yet first I was dismissed and now I must suffer this further humiliation." And fearful lest she should disclose her sorrow to the company, she held up her sleeve before her face to conceal the tears she could not stay.

But she was not hidden from Hotoke, who saw all and was smitten with sadness and compassion. "It is Gio," she said, turning to the Regent. "If you had only not sent her away-----. Please call her up here. Or, if not, dismiss me and I will go." But the Regent refused, as usual, to grant the latter plea and, realizing that all her entreaties were in vain, Hotoke left the hall.

The Regent then, after allowing some time to elapse, deigned to grant Gio an audience. "And how is Gio?" he then enquired, "And how has life seemed since------? As Hotoke seems lonely, please comfort her with an Imayo song and a dance." This was said cruelly to mock her for Hotoke was no longer present.

"Now that I have obeyed and am here," Gio mused sadly, "I will not disobey this further command." And summoning all her strength to withhold her tears she sang this Imayo:

> "The Blessed Lord who once wore mortal clay,
> Promised me I should merge with him one day
> When all go in to be His spirit's bride.
> Bitterness lies in being left outside."

Twice she sang the song, no longer able now to conceal her sorrow, so that all who were seated in the hall, princes, courtiers, the highest nobles and Samurai were moved. to tears.

Even the Regent acknowledged the justice of her complaint: "Marvelously sung," he declared, "and we understood too, the inner meaning of your song. Now I should like to see you dance, but," he added, "I have some business which prevents me. Hereafter," the cruel voice continued, "come often, to sing and dance and amuse Hotoke." Gio, unable to answer, went sadly out.

Arriving at her home, she cast herself down, musing half aloud, "I had made up my mind not to go, but in order not to disobey my mother's will, I went and suffered agony. Twice to have endured this torment is bitterness indeed. If I remain in this world I may be put to the torture again. I can go no farther. This day I must escape from this body."

The murmured words were heard by Gijo and her mother. "Sister," said the younger daughter, "if you leave this world, I will go with you." Stricken with deeper sorrow by what she heard, the mother sadly spoke: "I was wrong. My remorse is deep indeed for begging you to go when I did not know what you would have to suffer. If you end your life Gijo says she will join you, and if my two young daughters die first, of what use would the few sad years left me, be to your mother? No, I would not stay. I would end them with you.

"But to prevent one's mother from living out the appointed measure of her days is one of the five great sins. This world is but a transitory lodging place. Even shame heaped on shame is of little moment. Only the shadow of the long darkness of the coming world, that indeed is pain. If, in this world we become attached to things, in the after-life we must tread difficult paths in anguish."

Turned again by her mother's words, unable to bear their implication, Gio sadly submitted. "No," she said, "I am not willing to take upon me the burden of one of the five great sins. I said I would escape out of my life, from the pain which is pursuing me. I will not do so by killing this body. But if I remain in the capital my suffering would constantly be renewed. There is another path leading out of the world and it shall be mine."

Gio then, at the age of only one and twenty, became a nun. High in a mountain village in the recesses of Saga she built a hut of brushwood and lived there, calling upon the name of the Blessed Lord.

News of this, reaching the younger sister, Gijo, was not without its effect upon her. "I promised," she thought, "that I would go with my sister even unto death. How much more willing I should be to go with her now that she has merely set her face toward another life." So she, at the age of nineteen also became a nun and joining her sister in the mountain solitude she devoted herself to prayers for a better life.

Nor was the mother willing now to remain behind. "Since even these young girls," she considered, "have forsaken the world, how can I stay or suffer my gray hair?" And she cut off her hair and went to her daughters and with them breathed her invocations to the Blessed One, with prayers for a happier life in another world.

So the spring passed and summer came and faded. When the autumn winds began to blow, when the wild geese flew across the ford of heaven, when lovers wrote their longings on the flaming leaves, the three pitiful ones, by night, would gaze at the Herdsman and the Weaving Maiden, the lover-stars, drawing near to each other in the heavens.

And when the day had passed behind the blue hills they would watch the evening sky unfold the sunset vision; the Eternal Gardens, the Western Paradise, The Pure Land.

"Some day," they thought, "we shall be born there, in The Pure Land, at the end of the paths of sorrow." But they continued to tread those paths in a sadness deeper than their tears.

One evening, while the twilight was flowing into night, they had shut their latticed bamboo door and lighted the dim lamp. The three, mother and daughters, were already at their evening devotions when they heard an unprecedented sound. Someone had knocked on the door. The three nuns were at once overcome by fear. "Ah," they whispered, "it must be some demon come to still our prayers. What human being would come here to this mountain hut of brushwood? No one comes here even by day. The bamboo gate is too slight. If we do not unlatch it the lattice could easily be broken. We must open it. If anyone is there who would take our lives we shall pray to that Holy One who promised his suppliants a new birth in the Western Paradise. Then perhaps the Holy Assembly of Welcome who greet the faithful dead will come and lead us to the Eternal Gardens. Pray without ceasing to the Holy One."

So, strengthening each other, hand in hand, they threw wide the bamboo door.

It was no demon who stood there.

It was Hotoke.

"How can it be you?" Gio whispered, half to herself, "it must be a dream."

"If you will listen to my story," Hotoke's tears rose through her words, "it may seem to you merely like a dream. But if I do not tell you, I may always seem to you as one without human feeling. So I will tell you my whole heart from the beginning. I have not forgotten that I first went to the Regent's palace uninvited and was already dismissed when I was called back at your request. Then, because of the weakness of a woman before a man's will, against my own conscience I was powerless to stay your dismissal. I never forgave myself and I stand here ashamed. When I saw you go away, I knew that the same fate might fall upon me some day. I was never happy. And I saw, too, the lines you had written on the wall: "Autumn shall yield them all an equal fate," and I felt that it was true. Then when you were summoned again and sang the Imayo song, my position grew still more painful to me. For a while I did not know where you had gone. Then I heard that you had dedicated yourself to the Blessed One and were here absorbed in devotions.

"From that hour I was envious of you and continually begged the Regent for my freedom, but he always refused.

"Brooding over these things brought me to realize that the colors and splendors of this world are but dreams within a dream.

"What is pleasure? And what is prosperity?

"If it is difficult to achieve a human body, how much harder it is to live in this body and at the same time to do the Blessed Lord's will.

"If, lured by the shadow-glories of this life, I should fall into the Hells, how much more difficult it would be for me, toiling upward through renewed aeons of future lives, ever to ascend to Paradise.

"In this world, equally uncertain for young and old, we can not rely on our youth.

"The hour when this breath shall part forever from our dust, who knows it?

"Briefer than the gossamer fly that lives an hour in May, fleeter than the lightning, is our life.

"To be proud of the splendor that passes away and never to know of eternal life; is this understanding?

"At last, having considered these things, I made my escape secretly from the palace and came here."

With this she threw off the cloak she wore and revealed herself in a nun's habit.

"Now that I too have entered the Path," Hotoke continued, "I have come to beg your forgiveness. If you can grant it, we will supplicate the Blessed Lord together and together we may sit upon one lotus in Paradise.

"But if you cannot forgive me, I shall have to wander away, making my bed on moss or on the roots of the pine. Yet even then I shall worship the Blessed One to the end of my life," Hotoke held her sleeve before her face to hide her tears as she ended) "May He guide my feet to Paradise."

"Not even in my dreams," Gio answered, looking at Hotoke through her own tears, "did I imagine that your heart would turn to these things. I myself was the offender. Instead of seeing that my sorrows were the result of the disorder of this difficult world, I held you greatly to blame for them, thus suffering loss in this life and the next.

"But now that you have spoken these things, my bitterness toward you has faded away like the dew. Your words have freed me and, through this release, I do not doubt now that I shall at last be reborn in Paradise.

"And what could bring greater happiness than for us to tread the same path together for the rest of this life?

"It is a blessed thing to have entered the Path and I am thankful for having achieved it.

"Yet there was much to urge and press me toward it; the wounds I had suffered and my hatred of the world because of them.

"But you, who have been neither wounded nor rejected, and are only seventeen years old, have entered the Path of Light that leads away from this stained and clouded world, setting your desire on The Pure Land.

"I feel that yours is the true will towards the Great Light.

"How glorious is the Light! How warming all its rays!

"Let us offer our adorations together."

Thus, the four of them, with hearts turning wholly toward the Blessed One, morning and evening offered flowers and incense with devotions to their Lord.

It is said that they all, life by life, attained their desire for rebirth in Paradise.

In the registers of the temple Chokodo, built by the Emperor Go-Shirakawa, the spirits of the four, Gio, Gijo, Hotoke and the mother of the first two are enshrined together.

These are honorable things, to be cherished and to be yielded our deep reverence.

www.ingramcontent.com/pod-product-compliance
Lightning Source LLC
Chambersburg PA
CBHW040747020526
44118CB00040B/2719